Presented to:

_____

From:

_____

Date:

_____

99 Annoying Attributes of God

Ray Albrektson, Janet Kobobel Grant,
Alan Scholes, Gary Stanley,
Kirsten Wilson

*(Four out of the five of us admit to
having been annoyed with God at some point
in our lives—the other one is in denial.)*

HONOR HB BOOKS

Inspiration and Motivation for the Season of Life

COOK COMMUNICATIONS MINISTRIES
Colorado Springs, Colorado • Paris, Ontario
KINGSWAY COMMUNICATIONS LTD
Eastbourne, England

Honor® is an imprint of
Cook Communications Ministries, Colorado Springs, CO 80918
Cook Communications, Paris, Ontario
Kingsway Communications, Eastbourne, England

99 Annoying Attributes of God
Copyright © 2005 by Ray Albrektson, Janet Kobobel Grant,
Alan Scholes, Gary Stanley, and Kirsten Wilson

First Printing, 2005
Printed in the United States of America

Printing/Year
1 2 3 4 5 6 7 8 9 10   /   09 08 07 06 05

Cover Design: BMB Design/Scott Johnson
Interior Design and Photo © Chicken Little Creations
ISBN 156292303X

Scripture quotations appearing on pages 13, 19, 25, 31, 39, 55, 61, 69,
79, 91, 101, 117, 119, 125, 135, 139, 149, 151, 153 are taken from
Scripture taken from *The Message*. Copyright 1993, 1994, 1995, 1996,
2000, 2001, 2002. Used by permission of NavPress Publishing Group.

Scripture quotations appearing on pages 11, 15, 21, 37, 45, 67, 93, 105,
123, 131, 133, 155, 157 are taken from the Holy Bible, New Living
Translation, copyright © 1996 by Tyndale Charitable Trust. All rights
reserved.

Scripture quotations appearing on pages 29, 35, 43, 51, 73, 97, 99, 109,
111, 121, 147 are taken from the Contemporary English Version
Copyright © 1995 by American Bible Society. Used by permission.

Scripture quotations appearing on pages 9, 27, 53, 75, 85, 87, 129, 159
are taken from the HOLY BIBLE, NEW INTERNATIONAL
VERSION®. Copyright © 1973, 1978, 1984 International Bible
Society. Used by permission of Zondervan. All rights reserved.

Scripture quotations appearing on pages 113, 143, 160 are taken from
the New American Standard Bible®, Copyright © 1960, 1962, 1963,
1968, 1971, 1972, 1973, 1975, 1977, 1995 by The Lockman
Foundation. Used by permission. (www.Lockman.org.)

To our loved ones,
who put up with
our annoying attributes

Introduction

Ever wonder why God doesn't behave the way you think the Creator of the universe should? Or why his agenda seems to be at odds with yours? In case you haven't noticed, God can be rather, well, annoying at times. The following list of his troublesome traits helps to explain why the two of you don't always see eye to eye, so to speak.

God is annoying because

he often finds it
convenient to put me in
inconvenient situations.

The Lord provided a great
fish to swallow Jonah, and
Jonah was inside the fish
three days and three nights.

Jonah 1:17

God is annoying because

he takes everything
personally.

The King will tell them,
"I assure you, when you did
it to one of the least of these
my brothers and sisters, you
were doing it to me!"

Matthew 25:40

God is annoying because

he thinks what he wrote
two thousand years
ago still goes.

"Sky and earth will wear out;
my words won't wear out."

Matthew 24:35

God is annoying because

he's invisible.

"When he comes near,
I cannot see him. When he
moves on, I do not
see him go."

Job 9:11

God is annoying because

he's a perfectionist.

(Matt. 5:48)

God is annoying because

he gives Satan way
too much leeway.

(Job 1:12)

God is annoying because

he doesn't make it
easy to be good.

Anyone who wants to live all out for Christ is in for a lot of trouble; there's no getting around it.

2 Timothy 3:12

God is annoying because

he won't let me
take anything with
me when I die.

We didn't bring anything
with us when we came into
the world, and we certainly
cannot carry anything
with us when we die.

1 Timothy 6:7

God is annoying because

he won't take sides.

(Josh. 5:13–14)

God is annoying because

he didn't arrange the Bible
in a systematic way to make
it easy for me to extract
rules and principles without
having to bother him.

(John 5:39)

God is annoying because

he isn't particularly
interested in making
me look good.

It seems to me that God has put us who bear his Message on stage in a theater in which no one wants to buy a ticket. We're something everyone stands around and stares at, like an accident in the street.

1 Corinthians 4:9

God is annoying because

he doesn't accommodate
his schedule to mine.

"Lord," Martha said to Jesus,
"if you had been here, my
brother would not have died."

John 11:21

God is annoying because

he won't put my tasks
ahead of my relationship
with him—even when
there are things that just
have to get done!

The Lord answered,
"Martha, Martha! You are
worried and upset about so
many things, but only one
thing is necessary. Mary has
chosen what is best, and it will
not be taken away from her."

Luke 10:41–42

God is annoying because

he refuses to justify
himself to me.

"Where were you when I created the earth? Tell me, since you know so much!"

Job 38:4

God is annoying because

he's usually more
interested in my attitude
than in what caused it.

(Gen. 4:6–7)

God is annoying because

he never makes mistakes.

(Job 36:22–23)

God is annoying because

he doesn't ignore
my mistakes.

Where could I go to escape
from your Spirit or
from your sight?

Psalm 139:7

God is annoying because

he doesn't take the
easy way out.

Next the Devil took him
to the peak of a very high
mountain and showed him the
nations of the world and all
their glory. "I will give it all to
you," he said, "if you will only
kneel down and worship me."

"Get out of here, Satan,"
Jesus told him. "For the
Scriptures say, 'You must
worship the Lord your God;
serve only him.'"

Matthew 4:8–10

God is annoying because

he isn't swayed
by public opinion.

The Jews then said, "That clinches it. We were right all along when we called you a Samaritan and said you were crazy—demon-possessed!"

Jesus said, "I'm not crazy. I simply honor my Father, while you dishonor me. I am not trying to get anything for myself. God intends something gloriously grand here and is making the decisions that will bring it about. I say this with absolute confidence."

John 8:48–51

God is annoying because

he often thinks "no" is
a sufficient answer.

(Deut. 3:26)

God is annoying because

he always wins.

(Acts 5:38–39)

God is annoying because

his sense of mercy often
gets in the way of my
sense of justice.

Jonah was really upset and angry. So he prayed: "Our LORD, I knew from the very beginning that you wouldn't destroy Nineveh. That's why I left my own country and headed for Spain. You are a kind and merciful God, and you are very patient. You always show love, and you don't like to punish anyone."

Jonah 4:1–2

God is annoying because

he isn't impressed with
what I try to do for him.

Was it because of his good
deeds that God accepted him?
If so, he would have had
something to boast about. But
from God's point of view
Abraham had no basis at all for
pride. For the Scriptures tell us,
"Abraham believed God, so God
declared him to be righteous."

Romans 4:2–3

God is annoying because

he isn't impressed with
the verbal gymnastics
of my prayers.

(Matt. 6:7)

God is annoying because

he's way too generous
with my possessions.

(Matt. 5:40)

God is annoying because

he thinks my life is his.

(Matt. 7:24)

God is annoying because

he thinks I shouldn't
worry about anything.

(Phil. 4:6)

God is annoying because

he allows the wicked
to prosper.

Our God, how much longer
will our enemies sneer? Won't
they ever stop insulting you?
Why don't you punish them?
Why are you holding back?

Psalm 74:10–11

God is annoying because

he doesn't like it when
I want to get even
with somebody.

Do not say, "I'll pay you back for this wrong!" Wait for the LORD, and he will deliver you.

Proverbs 20:22

God is annoying because

he's long-suffering and
thinks I should be too.

"Don't run from suffering;
embrace it. Follow me and
I'll show you how."

Luke 9:23

God is annoying because

he is forgiving and
thinks I should be too.

(Eph. 4:32)

God is annoying because

he is omnipotent and
thinks I have no
business trying to be.

(Ex. 20:3)

God is annoying because

he thinks I should pray
for my enemies.

(Luke 6:27–28)

God is annoying because

he thinks humility is a
character quality I need.

(Luke 14:8–10)

God is annoying because

he thinks delayed
obedience is disobedience.

Then another said, "I'm ready to follow you, Master, but first excuse me while I get things straightened out at home." Jesus said, "No procrastination. No backward looks. You can't put God's kingdom off till tomorrow. Seize the day."

Luke 9:61–62

God is annoying because

he never loses an argument.

(Isa. 43:25–27)

God is annoying because

he thinks problems can
be a good way to
make me stronger.

(2 Cor. 4:16)

God is annoying because

he wants me to relax even when the situation clearly calls for stressing out.

(Matt. 6:31)

God is annoying because

he isn't interested
in satisfying my
curiosity about his
plans for other people.

(John 21:20–22)

God is annoying because

he's willing to do almost
anything to make me good
(and he thinks I ought
to be happy about it).

Dear brothers and sisters,
whenever trouble comes your
way, let it be an opportunity
for joy. For when your faith
is tested, your endurance
has a chance to grow. So let it
grow, for when your
endurance is fully developed,
you will be strong in character
and ready for anything.

James 1:2–4

God is annoying because

he expects me to
openly share the secrets
I'd rather keep hidden.

Make this your common
practice: Confess your sins to
each other and pray for each
other so that you can live
together whole and healed.

James 5:16

God is annoying because

he expects me to keep
secret the things I'd rather
openly take credit for.

(Matt. 6:1)

God is annoying because

he doesn't think my
anger is justified nearly
as often as I do.

(Jonah 4:9)

God is annoying because

he wants me to be
"glad" during the very
circumstances that
make me mad.

"God will bless you when others hate you and won't have anything to do with you. God will bless you when people insult you and say cruel things about you, all because you are a follower of the Son of Man. Long ago your own people did these same things to the prophets. So when this happens to you, be happy and jump for joy! You will have a great reward in heaven."

Luke 6:22–23

God is annoying because

he knows where I am no
matter where I try to hide.

When Samuel brought all the tribes of Israel near, the tribe of Benjamin was chosen. Then he brought forward the tribe of Benjamin, clan by clan, and Matri's clan was chosen. Finally Saul son of Kish was chosen. But when they looked for him, he was not to be found. So they inquired further of the LORD, "Has the man come here yet?"

And the LORD said, "Yes, he has hidden himself among the baggage."

1 Samuel 10:20–22

God is annoying because

he operates outside my
comfort zone and wants
me there with him.

(Ezek. 4:14–15)

God is annoying because

he knows what I'm thinking.

(Gen. 18:12–15)

God is annoying because

he's willing to allow me to
go my own way—even
when he knows I'll
end up in trouble.

There's a way of life that looks harmless enough; look again—it leads straight to hell.

Proverbs 14:12

God is annoying because

he doesn't appreciate
my rationalizations.

(Mark 7:10–12)

God is annoying because

he isn't wowed
by appearances.

(1 Sam. 16:7)

God is annoying because

he insists that the way to get
ahead is to take a backseat.

(Matt. 23:11–12)

God is annoying because

he thinks a healthy dose
of fear is good for me.

(Prov. 9:10)

God is annoying because

he won't give up.

"Suppose one of you has a hundred sheep and loses one of them. Does he not leave the ninety-nine in the open country and go after the lost sheep until he finds it?"

Luke 15:4

God is annoying because

he doesn't want me
to give up, either.

"When you pass through the waters, I will be with you; and when you pass through the rivers, they will not sweep over you. When you walk through the fire, you will not be burned; the flames will not set you ablaze."

Isaiah 43:2

God is annoying because

he won't let me
remain comfortable
with my own sin.

(Luke 5:8)

God is annoying because

he thinks comparing myself
favorably with others is a
lousy self-assessment test.

(Rom. 2:1–2)

God is annoying because

he isn't easy to follow.

"Don't look for shortcuts to God. The market is flooded with surefire, easygoing formulas for a successful life that can be practiced in your spare time. Don't fall for that stuff, even though crowds of people do."

Matthew 7:13

God is annoying because

he isn't worried enough
about either of our
reputations.

They asked him, "John's disciples are well-known for keeping fasts and saying prayers. Also the Pharisees. But you seem to spend most of your time at parties. Why?"

Luke 5:33

God is annoying because

he thinks being good is
way more important
than looking good or
feeling good.

(Amos 6:5–6)

God is annoying because

he often wants me
to act contrary to
the way I'm feeling.

(Matt. 5:41)

God is annoying because

he knows all about my
personal life and doesn't
hesitate to bring it up.

Jesus told her, "Go and
bring your husband."

The woman answered,
"I don't have a husband."

"That's right," Jesus replied,
"you're telling the truth. You
don't have a husband. You have
already been married five times,
and the man you are now living
with isn't your husband."

John 4:16–18

God is annoying because

he wants me to love
people I'd rather not.

"If you love only someone who loves you, will God praise you for that? Even sinners love people who love them."

Luke 6:32

God is annoying because

he isn't impressed with how clever I am.

Human wisdom is so tinny,
so impotent, next to the
seeming absurdity of God.
Human strength can't begin to
compete with God's "weakness."

1 Corinthians 1:25

God is annoying because

he doesn't think fixing
the problems in my life
ought to be the ultimate
test of his love.

(Rom. 5:8)

God is annoying because

he's immune to
the "everyone else is
doing it" argument.

(Eph. 4:17)

God is annoying because

his sense of timing
doesn't match mine.

When the apostles
were with Jesus, they kept
asking him, "Lord, are you
going to free Israel now and
restore our kingdom?"

"The Father sets those dates,"
he replied, "and they are
not for you to know."

Acts 1:6–7

God is annoying because

he's way too comfortable
with leaving things
open-ended.

(Gen. 12:1)

God is annoying because

he doesn't like my telling
him what to do.

(Job 38:4–7)

God is annoying because

he wants me to apologize
when I'd rather just let
offenses slide.

"If you are about to place your gift on the altar and remember that someone is angry with you, leave your gift there in front of the altar. Make peace with that person, then come back and offer your gift to God."

Matthew 5:23–24

God is annoying because

he wants me to trust him
just because of who he is.

The Lord says, "If you love me and truly know who I am, I will rescue you and keep you safe."

Psalm 91:14

God is annoying because

he has all the time
in the world.

Do not let this one fact escape
your notice, beloved, that
with the Lord one day is like a
thousand years, and a thousand
years like one day.

2 Peter 3:8

God is annoying because

he expects me to trust
him without knowing
all the particulars.

(1 Tim. 3:16)

God is annoying because

he's always kind, but
he isn't always nice.

(Rom. 2:4)

God is annoying because

he isn't worried about
my missing out on all the
stuff the world thinks is
important—and doesn't
want me to be either.

"Steep your life in God-reality,
God-initiative, God-provisions.
Don't worry about missing out.
You'll find all your everyday
human concerns will be met."

Matthew 6:33

God is annoying because

he isn't satisfied with letting
me be just a little better
than I am now.

Say a quiet yes to God and he'll be there in no time. Quit dabbling in sin. Purify your inner life. Quit playing the field. Hit bottom, and cry your eyes out. The fun and games are over. Get serious, really serious. Get down on your knees before the Master; it's the only way you'll get on your feet.

James 4:8–10

God is annoying because

he asks me to do things I
find embarrassing.

"Don't be ashamed of me
and my message among these
unfaithful and sinful people!
If you are, the Son of Man will
be ashamed of you when he
comes in the glory of his
Father with the holy angels."

Mark 8:38

God is annoying because

he isn't interested in
enabling my weaknesses.

He said, "My gracious favor
is all you need. My power works
best in your weakness." So now
I am glad to boast about my
weaknesses, so that the power of
Christ may work through me.

2 Corinthians 12:9

God is annoying because

he has a habit of confusing my part-time resolve with some kind of full-time commitment.

"Nothing halfhearted here;
you must return to God, your
God, totally, heart and soul,
holding nothing back."

Deuteronomy 30:10

God is annoying because

he sees right through me.

(Luke 6:46)

God is annoying because

he doesn't think it's good
enough for me to do
something just because
it's a "rule."

(Phil. 3:9)

God is annoying because

he drags things out
way too long.

The Jews gathered around him, saying, "How long will you keep us in suspense? If you are the Christ, tell us plainly."

John 10:24

God is annoying because

he refuses to give me
absolute proof of his
existence (so I can win
arguments with my
questioning friends).

"Abraham said, 'If they won't listen to Moses and the prophets, they won't listen even if someone rises from the dead.'"

Luke 16:31

God is annoying because

he set it up so that
my willpower alone
isn't enough.

No matter which way I turn,
I can't make myself do right.
I want to, but I can't. When
I want to do good, I don't.
And when I try not to do
wrong, I do it anyway.

Romans 7:18–19

God is annoying because

he always wants to lead.

Then Jesus went to work on his disciples. "Anyone who intends to come with me has to let me lead. You're not in the driver's seat; I am. Don't run from suffering; embrace it. Follow me and I'll show you how."

Matthew 16:24

God is annoying because

he isn't interested
in my excuses.

(Prov. 24:12)

God is annoying because

he keeps blowing away
the picture I have of him
just when I think I have
him figured out.

(John 6:18–20)

God is annoying because

he allows me to struggle and fail at the very things he could accomplish in the twinkling of an eye.

One man had been an invalid there for thirty-eight years. When Jesus saw him stretched out by the pool and knew how long he had been there, he said, "Do you want to get well?" The sick man said, "Sir, when the water is stirred, I don't have anybody to put me in the pool. By the time I get there, somebody else is already in."

John 5:5–7

God is annoying because

he isn't politically correct.

(John 14:6)

God is annoying because

he can be embarrassingly
affectionate.

(Luke 15:20)

God is annoying because

he's hard to please.

Without faith it is impossible
to please Him, for he who comes
to God must believe that He is
and that He is a rewarder of
those who seek Him.

Hebrews 11:6

God is annoying because

he invades my
personal space.

(John 13:5)

God is annoying because

He lets the consequences of
sin go on way too long.

(Ex. 20:5)

God is annoying because

he doesn't mind that
today is hard and expects
me to remember hard
times won't last.

These little troubles are getting us ready for an eternal glory that will make all our troubles seem like nothing.

2 Corinthians 4:17

God is annoying because

he doesn't make exceptions.

We've compiled this long
and sorry record as sinners
(both us and them) and proved
that we are utterly incapable
of living the glorious lives
God wills for us.

Romans 3:23

God is annoying because

he's not above using my
enemies to correct me.

God, you're from eternity, aren't you? Holy God, we aren't going to die, are we? God, you chose Babylonians for your judgment work? Rock-Solid God, you gave them the job of discipline? But you can't be serious! You can't condone evil! So why don't you do something about this? Why are you silent now? This outrage! Evil men swallow up the righteous and you stand around and watch!

Habakkuk 1:12–13

God is annoying because

he isn't interested in
building a consensus.

"There's trouble ahead
when you live only for the
approval of others, saying what
flatters them, doing what
indulges them. Popularity
contests are not truth contests—
look how many scoundrel
preachers were approved by
your ancestors! Your task is to
be true, not popular."

Luke 6:26

God is annoying because

he expects me to live up to
my own words.

David was furious. "As surely as the LORD lives," he vowed, "any man who would do such a thing deserves to die! He must repay four lambs to the poor man for the one he stole and for having no pity."

Then Nathan said to David, "You are that man!"

2 Samuel 12:5–7

God is annoying because

he decides when time is up.

"You have decided the length of our lives. You know how many months we will live, and we are not given a minute longer."

Job 14:5

God is annoying because

he is unwilling to
live up to my neatly
packaged image of him.

Since ancient times no one
has heard, no ear has perceived,
no eye has seen any God besides
you, who acts on behalf of
those who wait for him.

Isaiah 64:4

Conclusion

So when all has been said and done, is it okay to find God annoying? One old, battle-scarred warrior of the faith put it like this:

Evening and morning and at noon, I will complain and murmur, and He will hear my voice. He will redeem my soul in peace from the battle. (Ps. 55:17–18)

Nice to know that while God takes everything personally, he doesn't hold grudges. He does, however, hold hearts—wounded, troubled, and annoyed hearts. Bet he'd hold yours, too, if you'd ask him.